READY, SET, PLAY!

ALL THE FUNNEST, COOLEST GAMES **FOR KIDS!**

SCHOLASTIC

ALL THE FUNNEST, COOLEST GAMES FOR KIDS!

READY SET PLAY!

SCHOLASTIC

EDITOR IN CHIEF
Jon White

AUTHOR & EDITOR
Stephen Ashby

CONTRIBUTOR
Luke Albigés

LEAD DESIGNERS
Adam Markiewicz, Greg Whitaker

DESIGNERS
Steve Dacombe, Claire Evison, Philip Martin,
Alexander Phoenix, Will Shum

PRODUCTION
Alexandra Hoskins

ISBN 978-1-338-18994-0
10 9 8 7 6 5 4 3 2 1. 17 18 19 20 21
Printed in the U.S.A. 40
First printing, September 2017

Note to parents

We have specially selected all the games in *Ready, Set,
Play!* to appeal to young gamers and even played
them ourselves to ensure they're age appropriate.
These games will improve reaction speed, build
problem-solving skills, develop imagination and
creativity, and encourage teamwork. Many of them
are even educational, too (but you might not
want to mention that!)

CRASH BANDICOOT

Jump, spin, and slam your way to victory in three cool adventures in *Crash Bandicoot: N. Sane Trilogy*!

Staying safe and having fun

Video games are the most amazing things ever! Here are some top tips for having fun and staying safe when you're playing. Share them with your friends, too.

1 The games featured in this book are appropriate for you, but always check the rating of any new game before you play it. The ratings are there for good reasons, not to stop you from having fun.

2 Talk to a grown-up about your rules for gaming, and, ask how long you're allowed to play for.

3 If something happens in a game that you don't understand or don't like, always talk to a grown-up about it.

4 Tell a grown-up if you see anything that makes you feel unhappy or scared.

5 Always be nice to your friends and other players. Don't say or do anything that might make other players feel bad or make them unhappy.

6 Don't listen if other players are mean or make you feel sad. It's not your fault if someone says something bad. Let a grown-up know right away.

7 Don't download or install games or apps to any device

without checking with the person that owns it first.

8 If you're playing a mobile game when you're out and about, look where you're going to avoid accidents!

9 Remember to take regular breaks while playing games. Stop playing if you start to feel tired or sick.

10 Games are even more fun when played with friends, but be nice to your fellow players whatever the outcome. It's only a game!

CONTENTS

Top 5

50

30

120

36

94

46

Are you ready?

Games are a lot of fun! Battling through awesome levels with cool characters or playing with your friends is just awesome. But do you know all the best games? Well, let us help you out! This book is packed with facts, stats, tips, and tricks about the best games EVER!

Ready, Set, Play! will tell you all about the biggest characters in video games, from Mario to Skylanders. It will help you choose the best games to play with your friends and family in multiplayer, as well as the coolest games for you to explore on your own.

It doesn't matter which console you play on. If you have an Xbox, PlayStation, Wii U, Switch, 3DS, PC, or even a tablet or smartphone, there are lots of great games to enjoy. We've played the biggest and best games on them all, and can't wait to tell you all about them.

So, what are you waiting for? Ready, set, let's play!

20 BIGGEST GAMING MOMENTS

The coolest things that you can do in the biggest games

20 Create a kingdom
Dragon Quest Builders

As you build and upgrade villages in *Dragon Quest Builders*, more characters come and live there. Each building can be made in any way you want, so you'll be able to customize your town as you go.

19 Experience powered-up gaming
New consoles

Powerful new devices like the PlayStation 4 Pro offer amazing graphics that will blow your mind. Meanwhile, the Nintendo Switch lets you take console games on the move with its tablet screen. You can play it anywhere!

18 Race across the outback
Forza Horizon 3

Forza Horizon 3 takes players across Australia. Race family and friends through beautiful forests, over dusty sand dunes, and along golden beaches. You might find yourself stopping the race just so you can enjoy the view!

17 Win at Mario Party
Mario Party: Star Rush

Your friends don't need to own a copy of *Mario Party: Star Rush* for you all to play together. Start a game with them and race through each level, collecting cool characters and coins as you go.

16 Become a hero
Sonic Forces

There are three main characters in *Sonic Forces*—classic Sonic, modern Sonic, and you! Create your own custom *Sonic* character and you can sprint, roll, and slide along by his side!

15 Win the Star Cup
Mario Kart 8

The Star Cup in *Mario Kart 8* has four tracks. Mount Wario is the most epic thanks to the huge jumps and tight turns. If you can beat the 150cc difficulty, you'll feel like a champ!

20 Biggest Gaming Moments

14 Go back to a classic
Retro

Do your parents always tell you about the awesome games they used to play? There are plenty of standalone machines that let you play the best games from the past, so give them a try!

13 Score a last-minute winner
FIFA 17

Playing as your favorite soccer team is a dream come true. But one of the greatest achievements in *FIFA 17* is scoring in the last few seconds. Gooooal!

12 Learn new words, have fun!
Spellspire

Cast spells by spelling out words! As you climb the tower, monsters will get harder to defeat. But as you upgrade your gear and expand your vocabulary, you'll be able to reach higher floors. Aim for the top!

4,142

P O N I E S

Z O

M G

READY, SE

11 Go top of the leaderboard

Slither.io

Slithering around the screen in *Slither.io* is lots of fun. But if you want to be the biggest snake on the screen, you will need to gobble up lots of the glowing pellets. Get munching!

10 Become a Superhero

LEGO Marvel's Avengers

Tons of games let you play as your favorite heroes, but this one takes it one step further. Jump into LEGO *Marvel's Avengers* and you can create your own hero by choosing your own look and powers. Super!

9 Befriend a new Yo-kai

Yo-kai Watch

In *Yo-kai Watch,* making friends with the powerful creatures, called Yo-kai, is part of the fun. When you discover a powerful new Yo-kai, you can befriend them so they fight alongside you!

Adrenaline

Sgt. Burly   Jibanyan   Washo

8 Make new friends
Yooka-Laylee

Yooka-Laylee is about exploring a colorful world with two friends. But with so many funny characters to meet, you'll want to spend your time chatting, as well as jumping!

7 Set a high score
Super Mario Run

You can play *Super Mario Run* on your smartphone with just one finger, but that doesn't mean it isn't competitive! Your friends can set high scores that will appear in your game, so you can try to beat them!

6 Play with friends
Minecraft

Minecraft's competitive multiplayer modes let you play with your friends in fun mini-games. Try Tumble—digging out the ground from underneath other players so they fall down is really funny!

5 Find the best games
Roblox

The best thing about *Roblox* is that it has so many different kinds of games available. There's truly something for everyone here. And with millions of people playing, you'll always have friends to try out all the cool new games with!

4 Create a Skylander
Skylanders Imaginators

For the first time in a *Skylanders* game, you can create your own Skylander in *Imaginators*. There are millions of possible designs, and you can upgrade your Skylander as you play with new skills. Awesome!

3 Swing to win!
Arms

Arms isn't just a really fun game—it's good exercise, too. With a Switch Joy-Con in each hand, you punch the air to make the in-game characters do the same with their extendable arms. Just be careful of your surroundings while playing—don't break anything!

2 Experience VR

VR Headsets

VR (Virtual Reality) is going to take gaming to the next level. Players can put on a headset and feel like they're inside the game! In *Rez Infinite*, players fly through a multicolored world, destroying shapes. Amazing!

Oculus Rift

PlayStation VR

HTC Vive

1 Explore Alola

Pokémon Sun & Pokémon Moon

New *Pokémon* games are always a big deal, and *Sun* and *Moon* are no exception. With a whole new region to explore, new Pokémon to catch, and new evolutions for some of your favorite creatures, there's tons to do on the tropical islands of Alola. It's as much fun as going on a summer vacation!

Ask a Pro

There are so many awesome moments in gaming that it was nearly impossible to pick just 20! Don't forget, though, that the *real* best gaming moments aren't the ones you hear about from others—they're the ones you create for yourself. Whether it's an amazing creation, a stunning goal, or a tricky boss toppled, your own successes will feel best of all!

Introducing Mario

A platforming legend!

Mario is probably the most famous face in video games. Nintendo's cool character can do it all, from saving the princess to driving go karts, playing sports to baking, and even competing in the Olympics!

First appeared in: 1983
First game: Mario Bros.

Mario's first ever game saw the Italian plumber clearing out enemies in a New York sewer. It came out on Nintendo's first console, the NES, over 30 years ago!

Abilities:
★ Super jumping skills
★ Flying
★ Sports superstar
★ Driving
★ Dinosaur riding
★ Painting ★ Plumbing

Mario's top 3 sidekicks

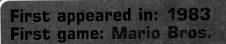

Luigi
Mario's brother is way taller than him. The brothers work together to save the day, but also like to go head to head.

Toad
There are loads of Toads in Mushroom Kingdom. They help Mario, and sometimes will even leap into action.

Princess Peach
Mario's girlfriend is often captured by the evil Bowser. When she's free, she loves playing sports with friends.

The Mario family
Did you know that the full names of the Mario brothers are actually Mario Mario and Luigi Mario? Confusing!

Power up!
Mario can pick up all kinds of power-ups to give him new skills. Picking up a Fire Flower will let him throw fireballs around.

Who is Jumpman?
Before he was known as Mario, our favorite hero was called "Jumpman" in the *Donkey Kong* arcade game.

In 2016, Mario appeared as part of the closing ceremony at the Olympic Games in Rio de Janeiro.

Mario races his friends across the Mushroom Kingdom in *Mario Kart 8*.

Mario's first proper appearance might look simple, but it's a platforming classic.

Super Mario Maker

Time to get creative

With *Super Mario Maker* you can build your own unique platforming levels, then share them with your friends! You can download tons of extra free levels, too. There's always a new one to try.

Highlight

Level clear!

Finishing a hard level and sliding down the flagpole is a great feeling. Check out your time, too. You might have even set a new world record!

TOP 3
level types

Tough jumps

1 When you make a level like this, make sure you show players the way to go. Use things like coins or arrows, and include enemies that are hard to get past.

Hidden routes

2 You can hide things like doors and other pathways through the level using items like a P-Switch. Try to test other players.

Boss challenge

3 *Mario* games are famous for their bosses, so try to mix things up a little bit. Put Bowser in an underwater level to really confuse people!

Did you know?

When your level is done, you can choose from three graphical styles, all from previous *Mario* games.

TIPS & TRICKS

PLAY ALL KINDS OF LEVELS

The best way to come up with new ideas is to be inspired by things others have made!

MAKE IT DIFFICULT

Don't make your levels too simple! Players are always looking for a challenge.

MAKE IT POSSIBLE

Don't include impossible jumps in your levels—it will only annoy players when they can't make it.

MAKE IT FUN!

Most of all, make sure your level is fun. Well-placed power-ups can give players a real boost.

Mario Kart 8

Ready? Set? Go!

Mario Kart has the cool characters and amazing levels of any Mario game. Then it throws in some power-ups, and puts you on a starting line in a go kart! From there, you can race against friends in this fast and fun game.

Did you know?
If you listen carefully as you drive through Shy Guy Falls, you'll hear the Shy Guys humming along to the music!

Highlight

Boost start!

You can get a boost right at the start of a race if you time it right. Just hold the accelerate button as soon as the number two drops!

TOP 3
tracks

Mount Wario

1 Wario's single-lap course is full of challenges. You'll leap from a plane, slalom down a slope, and skid through an icy forest as you battle it out for first place.

Did you know?

Mario Kart 8 is the first Mario Kart game in which Mario has an animated moustache that moves as he races!

Shy Guy Falls

2 In Mario Kart 8, the karts and bikes can drive up walls! Shy Guy Falls takes full advantage of this by having you race straight up an epic waterfall.

Toad Harbor

3 There are so many possible routes to take through Toad Harbor that you could take a different path every race! Try to find the fastest route possible to take first place.

TIPS & TRICKS

MASTER DRIFTING
Sliding sideways around corners will give you a small boost that can help win you a race.

USE SLIPSTREAMS
Follow right behind another racer and after a few seconds, you'll get a little speed boost.

FIND SHORTCUTS
Race the tracks alone to learn where the best shortcuts are, then you can beat your friends!

POWER UP!
Hold onto bombs and shells until other racers are about to jump a big gap—then throw them!

Super Lucky's Tale

Fantastic, Mr. Fox!

Want to explore an exciting and colorful world as a cute little critter? Then you're in luck, because you can! This fantastic adventure feels like a playable cartoon, with a cast of crazy characters to meet, plenty of goodies to collect, and some smart puzzles to solve.

Did you know?

Lucky first appeared in a free virtual reality game, given away to help promote the Oculus Rift headset.

Highlight

Making friends!

Lucky's world is full of friendly folks for you to get to know—it's hard not to instantly fall in love with these adorable, excitable little golem guys!

There are lots of hazards in Lucky's world, so keep your eyes peeled and try not to get your fuzzy friend hurt!

TOP 3
characters

1 Lucky
This intrepid little fox is the star of the show—you can tell from his awesome cape! You'll spend most time with Lucky, as he's the main playable character of the game.

2 Kooky Spookies
Don't be afraid, these ghostly guests are perfectly friendly! Be sure to compliment the bright white one on how great he looks in that fancy outfit!

3 The Worms
These hard-working worms are jolly and helpful. They're farmers by trade and are happy to lend our plucky hero a hand.

TIPS & TRICKS

BE PREPARED
Tricky "Jinx Levels" could pop up at any time, so make sure you're always ready for them!

MIX IT UP
There are many ways to defeat enemies—try bouncing on their heads, burrowing, or a tail thwack!

GETTING AROUND
Make good use of Lucky's double jump and dive moves. You'll be able to reach just about anything!

COLLECT COINS
Make like Mario and be sure to grab all the coins you see! You'll be a rich little fox in no time!

TOP 5 Cutest Characters

They're adorable!

Aww! Just look at these guys! Meeting adorable characters is one of the great things about playing games. The hardest part is deciding who is the cutest . . .

1 Chao
Sonic series

Sonic can feed, raise, and even race these friendly little creatures! His friend Cream also has a Chao companion called Cheese, who wears a cute little bow tie!

Did you know?

Depending on how you take care of a Chao, its appearance may change. Some of the transformations are really cool!

Pikachu

Pokémon series

This electric mouse has been the face of Nintendo's Pokémon series since it first began back in 1996. Don't hug Pikachu too tightly, though, or you might be in for a nasty shock!

3 Yarny

Unravel

Yarny from *Unravel* is a children's toy who travels across the land to get back to his owner. He will do anything to get back to his friend, which is why we love him!

Om Nom

Cut the Rope series

All Om Nom from *Cut the Rope* wants is candy, and he isn't afraid to ask. Wait until you see his sad face if you accidentally drop the candy . . .

5 Pikmin

Pikmin series

These tiny plant people just want to help you, and they all work together to do it! In the *Pikmin* games, they help you get back to your home, but you'll want to take them with you!

Q & A

What is a Pikmin?

These little plants grow on an alien planet called PNF-404. Captain Olimar crash-landed there during his vacation, and the Pikmin help him rebuild his ship!

What kind of game is *Pikmin*?

It's a mix of puzzles and action. Each Pikmin type has a different ability. Figuring out which one you need for each task is really important, especially if you meet an enemy!

LEGO Dimensions

Worlds collide!

Only LEGO *Dimensions* can bring together Superman, Harry Potter, and Sonic the Hedgehog in a single game. There are plenty more characters, too. Use them all to solve puzzles, fight monsters, and save the world.

Did you know?

There are 269 individual bricks in the LEGO *Dimensions* starter pack. That's a lot of building!

Highlight

Teamwork

Creating a team of your favorite characters is what makes the game so fun. Combine different powers to beat the game's hardest puzzles!

TOP **3** coolest characters

Sonic

1 Sonic is super fast! He can jump over big gaps without needing vehicles, and reach high areas thanks to his agility. His level pack also has some really cool platforming sections.

Did you know?

Playable characters from *Harry Potter* and LEGO *City* were added to the game in Wave 8.

Lloyd

2 This *Ninjago* master is quick, but he can also be stealthy to avoid traps. His vehicle can fly, too—he's a great all-arounder!

Scooby Doo

3 Scooby can follow scent trails, making him a useful member of your team. He can sniff out secrets in no time at all.

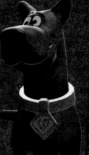

⏱ TIMELINE

SEPTEMBER 2015
GAME LAUNCHES

The Starter Pack launched, along with tons of extra characters to collect and use.

NOVEMBER 2015
WAVE 2

The first level pack, themed around *Doctor Who*, was released. New LEGO *Ninjago* characters appeared, too.

SEPTEMBER 2016
WAVE 6

The *Ghostbusters* Story Pack appeared, which retold the full story of the new movie.

FEBRUARY 2017
WAVE 7

Two more Story Packs launched, including The LEGO *Batman Movie*.

Crossy Road

Don't stop moving!

This smartphone sensation is easy to play, but beating your own high scores will be tough. The only goal is to get as far as you can. Sounds easy, but there are lots of obstacles in your way . . .

DID YOU KNOW?
The original version of the game was made in just 12 weeks, by three people.

Highlight

150
GREAT SCORE

High score!
Setting a high score feels great, but going back and beating it is even better. You can see your friends' scores marked on the level, too. Try to be the best ever!

TOP 3
coolest encounters

DINOSAURS

Play as the Tyrannosaurus Rex, and the whole level will change into a prehistoric party. Watch out for the stampedes of dinosaurs!

CROCODILES

Players that use the Kangaroo character will be transported to the Australian outback. Watch out for the hungry crocs in this level!

DID YOU KNOW?

You get a free gift in the game every few hours. You might get coins, or a new character!

PRESENTS

Unlock the Festive Chicken and you'll find gifts sprinkled throughout the level. Sadly, you can't get to the toys inside—they're really just in your way.

TIPS & TRICKS

TAKE YOUR TIME

Wait for your route to clear before you need to move. Don't panic and go too early!

BUT NOT TOO SLOW!

If you take too long to move, an eagle will fly down and swoop you back to the start.

GO BACK

Don't be afraid to move sideways or even backwards to find a better route through the level.

IGNORE THE COINS

Unless a coin is within a couple of spaces of you, ignore it. There's no point in risking it!

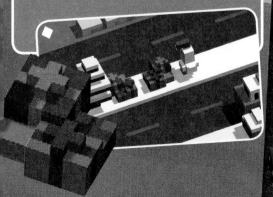

Introducing Sonic

He's fast!

Even your parents will have heard of Sonic. He's nearly 30 years old, but his games are still as fast and as fun as ever. He's had 3-D adventures, and has appeared in racing and sports games!

First appeared in: 1991
First game: Sonic the Hedgehog

Sonic speeds across grassy plains, through robotic factories, and into ancient tombs in this fast-paced platformer. It was designed to be a direct competitor to Mario's popular games in the early nineties. We love both!

Abilities:
- ⭐ Running fast
- ⭐ Driving
- ⭐ Sports superstar
- ⭐ Jumping
- ⭐ Collecting rings
- ⭐ Rolling into a ball

Sonic's top 3 sidekicks

Tails
Sonic's best friend is Tails the fox. He has two tails, which he can spin like helicopter rotors to fly!

Knuckles
Knuckles the echidna can glide and climb walls. He's a fierce fighter who defends the valuable Master Emerald.

Amy Rose
Amy the hedgehog is good friends with Sonic. They've saved each other's lives on several occasions in the series.

Sonic the Rabbit?!

Sonic was originally going to be a rabbit who could carry things with his ears, but the designers thought it would be too hard to animate.

The enemy

Sonic's main boss is called Dr. Eggman, but in Europe he was originally known as Dr. Robotnik.

Gotta go fast!

Sonic's speed isn't a super-power. It actually comes from his Power Sneakers that make him sprint really fast.

Watch for water

Sonic can't actually swim, but luckily he runs fast enough that he can skim across the water's surface.

This was Sonic's first adventure. At the time, it was the fastest game ever made!

Modern games, like *Sonic Generations*, mix 3-D action in with classic 2-D platforming.

Sonic Boom: Fire & Ice

Feel the speed!

Sonic's latest 3DS adventure brings the power of fire and ice to the series. Sonic can use fire to melt ice and light fuses, or switch to ice to freeze things. Plus, with his four friends to help, there's tons to do!

Did you know?

This game is the third spin-off from the *Sonic Boom* TV series after *Rise of Lyric* and *Shattered Crystal*.

Each character has a different skill. For example, Tails can fire a laser to defeat enemies.

Highlight

Elemental

Using the power of fire and ice while sprinting at high speed is awesome. You'll feel like a superhero as you turn water jets to ice.

TOP 3
key characters

01:34

Sonic

1 Of course! The hero must use the power of the elements to defeat Dr. Eggman and save his home! Be prepared for some serious speed.

Get used to this—Sonic spends most of the game speeding through levels as a blue blur.

Sticks

2 This badger lived alone for a long time, but is now friends with Sonic. She will do anything to help him, and her awesome boomerang skills are really useful.

Dr. Eggman

3 In *Fire & Ice*, Eggman has opened up cracks in the island that Sonic and his friends live on, and it's up to them to stop him before it's destroyed.

⏱ TIMELINE

2014
SONIC BOOM
This TV series sees Sonic and his friends living in a village on Bygone Island, defending it from threats.

2014
RISE OF LYRIC
As the team chase Dr. Eggman, they stumble across Lyric, an ancient evil snake. They have to stop him!

2014
SHATTERED CRYSTAL
Lyric captures Sonic's friend, Amy, and the team leap into action to save her.

2016
FIRE & ICE
Dr. Eggman's quest for Ragnium, a valuable element, damages Bygone Island, so the team must save the day.

TOP 5

TOP 5 Toughest Bosses

Beat the bad guys!

Beating the boss in any game is a real challenge, but these guys are the baddest bad guys. Beat them and you can count yourself among the very best gamers—they're the most evil bosses around!

1 Bowser
Mario series

This King of the Koopas wants to rule the Mushroom Kingdom. Mario has fought him dozens of times, and every time it's a real test of skill.

2 Emperor Kaos
Skylanders series

The evil Kaos will do anything to be in control, even if it means risking his own life. The Skylanders keep stopping him before he wins, but it takes teamwork and powerful characters to beat him.

Did you know?

Bowser is normally a bad guy, but sometimes he teams up with Mario if there is a threat that they both want to stop.

3 Lord Vortech

LEGO Dimensions

Vortech is the one who mixed up the universes in LEGO *Dimensions*. But by doing so they might all be destroyed, so you have to stop him! Each time you battle him is tougher than the last.

4 The Ender Dragon

Minecraft

If you go into The End without preparation in *Minecraft*, you'll meet your doom. The huge Ender Dragon spews out acid when he lands in the center of the arena, and can heal using the towers around him!

5 King Dedede

Kirby series

This penguin-like creature has been Kirby's nemesis since the first game, *Kirby's Dream Land*, in 1992. He calls himself the King of Dream Land, but he's really just a selfish, greedy bully with a giant mallet!

🎮 Ask a Pro

In most games, a boss has a weak spot that you need to aim for if you want to defeat them. It might be really obvious, like a big red blob on their back, or it might be more hidden. Focus on finding it, then figure out how to hit it to bring the boss down.

Introducing Steve

Minecraft magic!

You may have played *Minecraft* a lot, but you might not know that the character you're playing as is called Steve! This guy doesn't say much, but he's one of the best-known game characters in the world.

First appeared in: 2011
First game: Minecraft

One of the most recognizable games in the world, *Minecraft* began in its most basic form back in 2011. Since then it has sold millions of copies and has gotten some awesome updates.

Abilities:
★ Digging
★ Mining
★ Building
★ Crafting
★ Saying nothing
★ Farming

Steve's top 3 tools

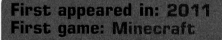

Diamond pickaxe

Getting diamonds is essential in *Minecraft*. The first thing Steve should make with them is this handy tool.

Leather armor

Protection is important in *Minecraft*. If Steve can find some cows, he can craft some cool leather armor.

Enchantment table

As Steve gains XP, he can build an Enchantment table to power up with new abilities like speed and fire resistance.

What's in a name?

The creator of *Minecraft* originally suggested the name "Steve" as a joke, when someone asked who the main character was.

Strength

Steve is super strong. He can knock down trees with his fists and carry hundreds of items with ease.

He's tall

Each block in *Minecraft* is a one-meter cube. Fans have measured Steve against them, and he is 1.85 meters. That's about six feet tall.

Meet Steve

The original character model for Steve had a beard, but it was removed when players thought it was a big smile!

Steve can play with his friends wirelessly using the recently added Realms add-on.

Multiplayer levels like this one are ready-made so Steve can just jump in and have fun with friends!

Minecraft

Just keep digging

Are you one of the tens of millions of people who have played *Minecraft*? If not, you're missing out. If you are, you know it's one giant playground where you can take on quests, beat bosses, build kingdoms, or just start a little farm and grow your own potatoes!

Highlight

Play with friends

Joining a multiplayer game with your friends and working together on a project is so much fun!

Did you know?
There are over 300 different items that you can find or make in *Minecraft*.

TOP 4 dangerous mobs

Did you know?
Minecraft has sold more than 25 million copies on PC and Mac alone!

Blaze

1 If you venture into the Nether, you'll find some of the toughest foes! Blazes hurl fireballs at you and can float away if you attack them. Being equipped with a bow and arrows is vital.

Charged Creeper

3 If a Creeper is struck by lightning, it will become charged! Charged Creepers explode with twice the range of a normal Creeper and do more damage, so stay away!

Elder Guardian

4 These odd bad guys guard ocean monuments. They do damage with their laser beam and spikes, which makes battling with them underwater even tougher.

The Wither

2 This terrifying mob can be made from soul sand and Wither skulls. It will fire projectiles at you, and can also fly. You'll need diamond weapons and armor to take on this deadly opponent.

TIPS & TRICKS

HOME COMFORTS
Making a base is a great idea. If you die while out exploring, you'll spawn back at your bed.

POWER UP
Collect as many experience points as you can, then improve your tools with an Enchantment table.

COOK IT UP
You can eat raw meat and eggs, but you'll restore more of your food bar if you cook food first.

GET CREATIVE
Start a new game in Creative mode if you just want to have fun building. You'll have unlimited blocks!

Did you know?

Creepers were made by accident when the game programmer turned a pig's body the wrong way by mistake!

There are some awesome multiplayer modes in *Minecraft: Console Edition*.

Holiday-themed skins are often released, plus you can download your own!

🕐 TIMELINE

MAY 17, 2009
MINECRAFT GOES PUBLIC
The very first version of the game was first made available to testers. It was incredibly basic.

JUNE 28, 2010
THE ALPHA
The first major update to the test version added new mobs, redstone circuits, and more!

NOVEMBER 18, 2011
FINAL RELEASE
The official release added the Ender Dragon, and there have been dozens of updates since.

OCTOBER 13, 2015
STORY MODE!
Minecraft: Story Mode was released. It told a brand new story in the *Minecraft* world!

You'll find villages dotted around, with characters that will trade with you.

Ask a Pro

Beating the Ender Dragon, the huge, deadly boss, is all about preparation. You'll need the best armor and weapons, and ideally an enchanted bow. Take plenty of potions with you, and focus your attacks on the crystals that give the dragon its health back before you aim for the dragon itself!

Did you know?

The first version of the game was called *Cave Game*, but only for six days!

Q & A

What do I need to play Minecraft?

You can play on almost any device, whether it's a home console like an Xbox One or PS4, a tablet, or your home computer. *Minecraft* is available on them all!

What's the story?

There isn't one! That's one reason why people love it. You're in charge. You can do whatever you want, whether it's building castles or exploring the world!

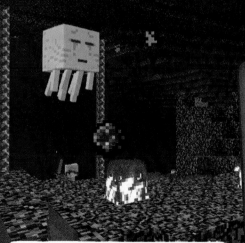

The Nether is a dangerous world full of scary mobs, but it holds useful items, too.

Minecraft: Story Mode

Quite a tale to tell . . .

This series breaks new ground for *Minecraft* by adding a story to a game that was just about digging and building. Here, you take control of Jesse and his friends as they save the *Minecraft* world from a monster . . .

Did you know?

In *Episode 6: A Portal to Mystery*, you might recognize a few voices, like DanTDM and Stampy!

Highlight

If you play *Minecraft*, you'll recognize all of your favorite monsters as you go.

Upgrading

As you progress through the story, you'll get new armor and more powerful weapons. You'll look and feel like a true hero by the final episode!

TOP 3
coolest characters

Jesse

1 The game's hero is a fan of all things *Minecraft*. When an accident unleashes the scary Wither, Jesse must find five heroes to help save the world.

Petra

2 Petra is always the first one to defend her friends. She is also really good at spotting things the other team members have missed. She is a strong fighter, too, and is competitive.

Reuben

3 Jesse's pet pig is also his or her best friend. You can ask him advice in the game, but he won't really say much. Still, he's one of the funniest characters in the game!

TIPS & TRICKS

KEEP TALKING
The more times you talk to people, the more information you'll get. Be chatty!

DON'T PANIC
There will be times when you have to fight off Creepers. Don't panic, just take them on one at a time.

CRAFTING
It never hurts to upgrade your gear. Make a stronger stone sword when your wooden one breaks.

REPLIES MATTER
Some characters will remember if you make them happy or sad, so think about what you say.

Kingdom Hearts III

All your favorite heroes

Sora returns in *Kingdom Hearts III*, with Goofy and Donald Duck by his side! You can use Disney heroes, and even some of Disneyland's famous rides, to stop the evil Master Xehanort.

Your Keyblade can transform into all kinds of things, like this huge launcher!

Highlight

Epic bosses

There are some massive monsters you'll need to take on in the latest game. You can climb them as Sora, or use the Keyblade's abilities to defeat them.

TOP 3 abilities

Pegasus Chariot

1 Sora's Keyblade can transform into Hercules' magical chariot, which is pulled by a flying horse! It's a really powerful attack.

Pirate Ship

2 Sora can summon theme-park rides to help him in his quest. This huge pirate ship quickly spins around to damage enemies around him.

Mad Tea Party

3 In this Summon, Sora, Goofy and Donald jump into teacups that spin around and damage enemies that get caught up in the chaos. Just don't get dizzy!

TIMELINE

The evil Ansem uses Disney villains to try and open the door to Kingdom Hearts.

Sora searches for Riku and Mickey, but must travel to a scary castle and defeat Organization XIII to do it.

The Organization returns, wanting to reclaim their hearts using the power of Kingdom Hearts.

Sora and Riku study to gain the Mark of Mastery, which will allow them to become Keyblade Masters.

Yo-kai Watch

Make some new friends!

Have you discovered the mysterious Yo-kai yet? In Yo-kai Watch, you make friends with these strange creatures, and battle other Yo-kai to stop them causing mischief!

Did you know?

There are three Yo-kai Watch games, but the third is only available in Japan at the moment.

Highlight

Cadin   Jibanyan   Tattletell

Soultimate!

Each Yo-kai has a unique skill, called a Soultimate. When your Yo-kai's Soultimate power is charged, it can completely change the course of a battle!

TOP 3 coolest characters

Whisper

1 Whisper is the first Yo-kai you meet, and the most helpful! He knows tons about Yo-kai, so he can always help out with information.

Baddinyan

2 Fuse Jibanyan with one of the Roughraffs in Uptown Springdale and you'll get Baddinyan! His special attacks are really useful, and he's super fast, too.

Dragon Lord

3 Fuse a Draggie with a Dragon Orb and it'll turn into Dragon Lord! This powerful Yo-kai has some really strong attacks, and can improve the abilities of its allies as well.

TIPS & TRICKS

STAY FOCUSED

Concentrate on the main quest at first to get the intro done. It's quite long, so stick with it!

POWER UP

Fuse two Yo-kai, or fuse a Yo-kai with a special item, to evolve them and make them more powerful.

KEEP WATCH

If your Yo-kai meter pings, a Yo-kai is near! Look around objects like trees to find them.

BUILD A TEAM

You don't have to befriend every Yo-kai, so focus on a strong team.

Dragon Quest Builders

A whole new world . . .

Does creating your own world sound fun? Then you'll love *Dragon Quest Builders*! In each level, you'll need to build things to create a town. But it's up to you how big things are and how it all looks . . .

Highlight

The evil Dragonlord destroyed everything in the kingdom, so you need to rebuild it.

Community

You're the only one in the world of Alefgard that can build, so there are lots of homeless characters. Creating towns for the people you meet is a great feeling.

TOP 3 things to do

Mining

1 Before you build your town, you'll need materials. Find the blocks you need and mine them. Then you can take them back and start getting creative!

Did you know?

The game looks similar to *Minecraft*, but it has its own style, and a story that drives you to get creative.

Fighting

2 There are plenty of impressive monsters around the game world. You'll need to fight them as part of quests, or just to access new materials.

Building

3 As you build more structures, characters will start to move into your town. Soon, you'll have your own small community to take care of and build for.

TIPS & TRICKS

Building structures out of dirt will help you to progress quickly. You can upgrade them with stone later.

Before you go out of your town to gather resources, ensure you have plenty of tools and food!

Unless your current quest is important, you should sleep at night to avoid the annoying ghosts.

Crops grow every day, so plant them at night and they'll be ready to harvest in the morning.

Cut the Rope

Awesome puzzling fun

You think feeding your pets is easy, right? Maybe even a little boring? Well, meet Om Nom! He's always hungry, and it's your job to feed him candy. Watch out, though—this is not as easy as it sounds!

Did you know?
There are 1,275 stars to collect in the original *Cut the Rope* game across 425 levels!

There are new ideas in every box, like this sleepy level where you have to wake up Om Nom to feed him.

Highlight

6	7	8	9	10
11	12	13	14	15
16	17	18	19	20
21	22	23	24	25

Box complete!

The feeling of grabbing those last stars in a tough level is great, but it's when you see this screen that you know that you've really mastered the game.

TOP 3 level challenges

Conveyor belts

The final box in the first *Cut the Rope* game has this tricky addition. Items like bubbles and ropes are attached to them, so you need to move things around to make everything work.

Currents

In *Cut the Rope: Magic*, flowing currents will pull the candy (and Om Nom) around the level. Figure out how to get the two together so Om Nom can eat!

Time travel

You get to meet Om Nom's ancestors in *Cut the Rope: Time Travel*. Moving time forward and backward will change the level, so plan each change carefully.

TIPS & TRICKS

In *Cut the Rope 2*, you'll get free hats as you play that you can put on Om Nom. Cute!

Once you've completed a level, play it again to get a good time for bonus points.

Tap the candy on the main menu screen and it will change into a doughnut or cupcake in every level.

There are hidden pictures in the backgrounds of some levels. Tap everywhere to find them!

TOP 5
Best Puzzle Games

Brain training!

Games aren't just fun—they can also be a great workout for your brain! Puzzle games are usually quite quick, making them ideal when you only have a short time to play.

1 Angry Birds

One of the most successful mobile games ever, and with good reason! Figuring out which birds to use and where to aim them in order to cause maximum mayhem is only half the battle—you'll still need skill to pull off the shot.

DID YOU KNOW?

Tetris is the best-selling game of all time, reportedly having sold close to 500 million copies across all versions!

2 Puyo Puyo Tetris

Two all-time classic puzzle games, together at last! Make lines to clear the board, group Puyos together to create combos, or do both at once in the new crossover game modes.

3 Bejeweled

A simple match-three puzzler, but one that can be extremely fast once you learn to spot patterns. The game has been so popular that Hasbro even turned it into an actual board game!

4 Picross

Use number clues to place blocks and form pictures. It seems complicated at first, but you'll soon figure out how to solve the puzzles. Later ones can be really tricky though!

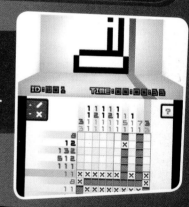

5 Pokémon Shuffle

Swipe Pokémon into groups of three or more to attack! The Pokémon that appear change based on your party. To do well, you'll need to bring Pokémon that can hit the defender's weakness.

Ask a Pro

Although every puzzle game uses different rules, there's a lot of crossover in the kinds of patterns that tend to be the most useful. By playing lots of puzzle games, you'll be able to get better at all of them!

TOP 5
Funniest
Characters

Get ready to laugh!

Games don't have to be serious or difficult to be good. In fact, funny games are often a lot more fun to play! That's why we love these characters—they make us laugh out loud every time they're on-screen.

1 Flynn

Skylanders series

This friendly pilot is clumsy, accident-prone, and always saying silly things. We also love Flynn because he always has our back.

Did you know?

Flynn has appeared in every *Skylanders* game, and also starred in Spyro's own game series.

2 Reuben
Minecraft: Story Mode

It's hard to be funny when you're a pig, but Reuben manages it! Jesse's companion is always making us giggle, especially when he puts on weird masks!

3 Ratchet
Ratchet & Clank

You might not expect a talking Lombax to be funny, but Ratchet and his friends tell jokes that will have you laughing hysterically.

4 The Rabbids
Rayman series

These weird creatures are like a cross between Minions and the Mad Hatter. They shout and scream a lot, get into all kinds of odd situations, and wear hilarious costumes.

5 Benny
LEGO games

Benny hops around with excitement when he's finally allowed to build a spaceship, and shouts "SPACESHIP!" as he does it. It's adorable—and really funny!

Q & A

How can I play as Benny?
Benny appears in *The LEGO Movie Videogame*, and he's also a playable character in LEGO *Dimensions*. However, you'll need to buy his minifigure to use him in-game.

Why do I recognize Benny?
He was the hilarious Master Builder in *The LEGO Movie*. He always wanted to build spaceships to help his friends!

Play Together!

Get into your favorite games with friends

Games are a lot of fun when you play on your own, but there's nothing better than sitting down to play with friends or family. Whether you're laughing with them in the same room, or playing with your friends online, multiplayer games are one of the best gaming experiences. Some games will have you working together to solve problems, while others will have players competing to set the fastest time or highest score. Just remember to always check with your parents before playing online, and never share any personal information online.

WHAT YOU WILL NEED

Everything you need to start playing with friends

TV

If you're playing with friends or family in the same room, you'll likely be gathered around one screen. Any kind of TV works as long as you can see what your character is doing.

Controllers

If you're playing online you'll only need one controller, but local multiplayer games often have two or more players, so extra controllers are really useful.

Console

For online games, your console will need to be connected to the Internet. For local multiplayer, though, it just needs to be hooked up to the TV for the fun to start!

PLAY WITH FRIENDS AT HOME

Get ready for local multiplayer fun

Gaming is awesome when you're sharing it with friends sitting next to you.

These multiplayer tips are what you need to have a great local multiplayer game!

Local multiplayer tips

Talk it over

If you're playing a co-op game, keep talking to the other players to let them know where you are and what you're doing. This will make it easier to play well as a team!

Don't cheat

If you're losing, you might be tempted to distract your friend from the game to try and catch up. This is a cheap tactic—just play hard and do your best to win!

No peeking!

If you're playing a game where you can see your opponent's view, it's tempting to see what they're doing and use it to your advantage. Don't do it, just focus on your own game!

THE BEST LOCAL MULTIPLAYER GAMES

Fun with your friends!

LEGO Dimensions
Universes collide in this game! You'll be placing LEGO minifigures on a special pad to see characters appear in the game. Team up to create the ultimate squad!

Mario Party 10
This is the craziest board game you'll ever play! Jump in with up to three of your friends and family to try and earn the most stars as your favorite *Mario* characters.

Overcooked
Work with up to three others to cook burgers, pizzas, and more. Crazy kitchens, with mice that steal food, make this hilarious and completely manic!

FIFA 17
This soccer simulator is even more fun with friends. Pick your favorite team from over 650 and outplay your opponent in the most realistic soccer game ever.

MORE LOCAL MULTIPLAYER GEMS

More fun with friends!

Mario Kart 8

Racing games don't get any crazier than *Mario Kart*. The eighth release of the game introduces flying karts that can drive up walls and upside down. This is a multiplayer classic.

Did you know?

Mario Kart 8 Deluxe is now available on Nintendo Switch, with new tracks and racers.

Minecraft

You can play with up to four people on one TV using the console version of the game. This is great if you want to work together on a building project, or just start a new adventure.

Trackmania Turbo

Two players control one car in one of *Trackmania Turbo's* many multiplayer modes. But they both need to steer the same way to turn! The split-screen mode also has some cool stunt modes.

Play Together!

◯ 2687
4/20

Yoshi's Woolly World

Two Yoshis can work together to find secrets. You can even swallow your teammate and spit them out! If you're feeling nice, this will give them a jump boost. If you're feeling mean, it will help you grab gems first!

Did you know?

You can design your own characters in *#IDARB*, and create your own music in the game.

00:28
ROUND 2

@idarbwire #K23V

ox One. #IDARB Battle of Breakfast! full size image > http://t.co.twCKAYNG_N http://t.co.kgmW

Q & A

#IDARB

#IDARB is bizarre, but a lot of fun. Two teams jump through an arena trying to score goals. But tackling, special moves, and even unique rules randomly come into play, so it's always hard to predict who will win!

How do I know if a game has local multiplayer support?

If you download a game, the multiplayer details will be listed on the store. If you have a game on disc, the back of the box will tell you about playing locally or online.

Do I need lots of controllers?

You might need more than one, but some games let you take a turn, then pass the controller on to the next person.

PLAY WITH FRIENDS ONLINE

Play with friends and family wirelessly

Sometimes, your friends can't be with you. But that doesn't mean you can't enjoy multiplayer games. Online modes help you play with your friends, without a giant couch!

Tips for online play

Add your friends

Your friends will have special online names or codes, which you can use to add them to your Friends List. You'll be able to see if they're online so you can join in!

Create a party

When you and your friends are all online, you can create a "Party." This will put you all in an online group, so you can play games and chat together.

Talk to your friends

If you have a headset connected to your console, you can talk to your friends as if they are there with you! This is great for deciding what you're going to do next.

THE BEST ONLINE MULTIPLAYER GAMES

Amazing games to try

Did you know?

Forza Horizon 3 includes cars made by 80 companies, including Ferrari & McLaren.

Splatoon

Getting messy is fun, and that's what *Splatoon* is all about! You must cover as much of the level as you can in your paint, as your friends try to do the same.

Forza Horizon 3

Team up with friends and you can complete missions in some of the world's most beautiful cars. Or, if you want, you can race each other through jungles, or explore the Australian landscape together.

Rocket League

This game puts six rocket-powered cars into a huge arena and drops a big soccer ball in. Your team's job is to score! *Rocket League* is fast-paced, as you and your friends work together to win.

Did you know?

Rocket League isn't just soccer—there are modes based on basketball and hockey, too!

Ask a Pro

If you don't have a headset or microphone to chat with your friends, don't worry. In some games, like *Rocket League*, you can send short messages to your friends by pressing a button on the controller. Tell them what to do, or congratulate them when they score a point!

Introducing Pikachu

We choose you!

This lovable electric mouse is the famous mascot of the *Pokémon* TV series and movies as Ash Ketchum's sidekick and friend. But Pikachu is also a powerful Pokémon in the game series, too!

First appeared in: 1996
First games: Pokémon Red and Pokémon Blue

The first ever *Pokémon* games involved exploring the Kanto region to become a Pokémon master and defeat the Elite Four with a team of powerful friends.

Abilities:
* Thundershock
* Agility
* Quick Attack
* Double Team
* Adorable face

Pikachu's top 3 Pokémon buddies

Squirtle

Squirtle is one of the three starter Pokémon from the first *Pokémon* games. In the TV series, Ash and Pikachu made friends with a cool Squirtle.

Snorlax

This sleepy Pokémon isn't just one of Pikachu's buddies—he's also a fan favorite. He is suprisingly agile and caring, and protects Pikachu.

Noivern

Noivern is a bat Pokémon that first appeared in *Pokémon X and Y*. In the TV series, Pikachu makes friends with Noivern after it hatches from an egg.

What does it mean?

Pikachu's name means something! "Pika" is the Japanese word for the sound of crackling electricity, while "Chu" means mouse.

Male or female?

A female Pikachu will have a notch in its tail, so it looks a little like a heart shape; while a male's tail is straight and flat.

Pokémon GO starter

If you want to catch Pikachu first in *Pokémon GO*, you can do it! Just keep walking away from the three starter creatures until this guy appears.

Mascot competitor

Originally, the mascot for the *Pokémon* series was going to be a Pokémon called Clefairy. Luckily, though, Pikachu was a fan favorite!

Dress up

In *Pokémon Omega Ruby* and *Alpha Sapphire*, Pikachu can dress up in five cute outfits as part of a costume contest.

Soon after *Pokémon Red* and *Blue*, *Pokémon Yellow* launched with Pikachu as your companion from the start.

You can do battle with some other famous Pokémon in the arcade title *Pokkén Tournament*.

Pokémon Sun & Moon

A paradise full of fun!

The latest *Pokémon* games give you a new area to explore—the tropical islands of Alola. Each version is slightly different, so whether you play *Sun* or *Moon* is up to you!

Did you know?

Pokémon can now have a super powerful Z-Move that can be used when battling to get a boost!

Highlight

Trial Start

The Trials

Rather than Pokémon Gyms, Alola has seven trials that you can complete to gain new abilities and skills. They usually end in a battle, though, so get your Pokémon ready.

TOP 3 new Pokémon

Rockruff

1 This little puppy will be one of the first Pokémon you come across. It will evolve into different forms depending on whether you play *Sun* or *Moon*.

Rowlet

2 It's tough to choose a favorite from the three new starter Pokémon. Rowlet is a great choice, though, because it has Flying type moves that are really useful early in the game.

Lunala

3 This legendary Pokémon is incredibly powerful, and is the only known Pokémon who can learn the Moongeist Beam attack. You can only catch one in *Pokémon Moon*.

⏱ TIMELINE

1996

RED & BLUE
The first *Pokémon* games ever introduced us to this amazing series.

2006
DIAMOND & PEARL
The series moved to the DS for the first time and introduced more Pokémon to capture.

2010
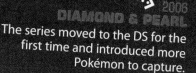
BLACK & WHITE
This was a major step forward in the series, with a new 3-D world to explore.

2013
X & Y

The power of the 3DS meant these looked even better than the 3-D world of *Black* and *White*!

Pokémon GO

Catch 'em all!

This mobile sensation challenges players to walk around their neighborhoods and catch Pokémon in the real world. It's got tons of creatures to catch and secrets to find! Just watch where you're going . . .

Did you know?

At launch, Pokémon GO was the most-used smartphone app in the whole world!

Highlight

Medal winner!

Congratulations! You earned a medal!

Catch 200 Water-type Pokémon.

You will earn medals like these when you complete certain tasks. The best thing is that as you earn more medals, it gets easier to catch certain Pokémon!

TOP 3 things to do

Visit PokéStops

1 There should be lots of these around you. Walk up to a blue PokéStop and you can spin it—this will give you supplies like Poké Balls, Potions, and Eggs.

Catch Pokémon

2 Pokémon will appear near you. Tap one and throw a Poké Ball to try and capture it. Some Pokémon will be harder to catch, just keep trying!

Conquer Gyms

3 If another team is holding a Gym, you'll need to battle to win it for your team. Once it's yours, you can claim PokéCoins and use them to buy more useful supplies.

TIPS & TRICKS

USE LURES
You can put a lure on a PokéStop to attract more Pokémon to that area for 30 minutes.

PLAY SAFELY
Always have an adult with you when you go out Pokémon hunting, and look where you're walking!

IN THE RING
Aim to land your Poké Ball inside the ring when you throw it for an XP bonus.

TURN AR OFF
The Augmented Reality (AR) mode puts Pokémon in the real world, but turning it off makes catching them easier.

TOP 5
Unique Games to Try

One of a kind

You've probably played lots of sports and action games, but there are other genres to try, too. Here are some unique games that are a ton of fun!

1 Overcooked

Up to four players can join in on this action-packed cook-off! You work together to make meals in weird kitchens. Can you keep your cool when mice steal your ingredients?

DID YOU KNOW? Two people can play *Overcooked* at the same time with just one controller. Things might get messy, though . . .

2 Grow Up

Meet BUD, a robot built to climb! When he lands on a mysterious planet, he must clamber up structures to reach parts of his spaceship. It's all about flying, jumping, and climbing.

3 Fez

Fez is about Gomez, who thinks he lives in a 2-D world. When a strange item reveals that the world is 3-D, it changes the game and creates great puzzles!

4 Scribblenauts

In *Scribblenauts*, you have to come up with a solution to a problem. If you type a word on the screen, that thing will appear. So if you want a robot dinosaur, you can make one!

5 Journey

In *Journey*, you play as a mysterious and silent creature who travels across an incredible world. It is an amazing and beautiful game.

🎮 Ask a Pro

Let your imagination loose in *Scribblenauts*. If your task is to save a cat from a tree, for example, you can do all kinds of things to do it. You could make a ladder to climb, create an ax to cut the tree down, or spawn a superhero to help you!

Roblox

So many games in one!

The world of Roblox is super fun—there are so many different things to try! You can play thousands of games, all created by members of the community. When you're older, maybe you can start making your own games, too!

Did you know?

The game was first released way back in 2006, but it has grown and evolved hugely over the years.

Highlight

There's always something new!

Every time you play *Roblox*, you'll find cool new games to try. There will also be updates to your favorites that make them even better. Check back often!

TOP 3 Best Games

Bird Simulator

1 Take to the skies as any of the awesome feathered friends on offer. Just roam around freely, fly with friends, or even take on tricky challenges!

Mini Golf!

2 No prizes for guessing what this game is! There are 90 holes to challenge across a number of environments, which is hours of fun. Can you get a hole-in-one?

Disaster Warning:
Fire! Keep distance from the fire

Natural Disaster Survival

3 Anything can happen! You need to react to whatever the game throws at you. It could be rising tides, falling objects, or even scary zombies! Work together to get to safety.

TIPS & TRICKS

Not all games are competitive. In those that aren't, try to help other players. Hopefully, they will help you back!

Roblox is home to all kinds of different experiences. Play a lot to help grow your gaming skills.

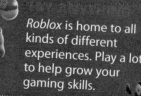

Don't forget to dress up your character to make them look as cool as possible!

Every game is different, so be sure to check out the rules when you start a new game.

Splatoon
Make a mess!

G etting messy is fun, and mess is what *Splatoon* is all about! The game throws you into a level with your team, and you have to cover it in paint. The opposing team will do the same, so prepare for battle!

Did you know?

Nintendo planned for the animals to be rabbits rather than squid. They soon realized squid were much . . . well, splattier!

Highlight

Team up

Getting together with your friends and jumping into a battle feels great, especially if you can work together with your team to win the game!

TOP 3 levels

Walleye Warehouse

1 This long, narrow level is great because it pushes the teams together into the central area for a battle. However, there are some sneaky passages at the side . . .

Camp Triggerfish

2 This awesome floating camp isn't all fun. You'll need to watch out for the water below. Be ready for the floodgates to open so you can access the new areas they unlock.

Kelp Dome

3 There isn't really anywhere to hide in this open map, so you need to look out for enemies at every turn. Splat Zones mode is particularly fun in this cool arena!

TIPS & TRICKS

USE YOUR SPECIAL
When the meter in the top-right is full, you can unleash your Special. Keep an eye on it.

ESCAPE!
Lay down ink up to a grate, go into squid form, and press X to drop through.

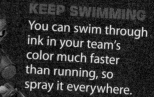

KEEP SWIMMING
You can swim through ink in your team's color much faster than running, so spray it everywhere.

BUDDY UP!
Work together with your allies and you'll do a lot better than if you try to go it alone. You'll paint areas quicker, and be safer if an enemy appears.

TOP 5
Best
Free
Games

Free for all!

Some of the best games around are available for free. Here are five of our favorite free titles to download and play. Give them all a try!

1 Alto's Adventure

This endless snowboarding game is all about doing tricks and jumps, and getting the best score possible without crashing. The game is really beautiful, and Windows 10 users can download it for free.

DID YOU KNOW? Some of the challenges in *Alto's Adventure* are pretty funny. At one point, you have to chase a runaway llama—which isn't easy!

2 Frozen Free Fall

Princesses Anna and Elsa have their own puzzle game! You'll see all your favorite *Frozen* characters in this game, available for smartphones, tablets, and consoles.

3 Disney Crossy Road

This game has you crossing busy roads, toy boxes, and African plains as your favorite Disney characters. Get as far as you can, and unlock hundreds of characters as you play!

4 Sonic & All-Stars Racing Transformed

This smartphone game has all your favorite SEGA heroes, like Sonic and NiGHTS, plus characters like Wreck-It Ralph! You can race around crazy courses.

5 Powerstar Golf

This golf game is chilled-out sports fun on the Xbox One. The free version is limited, but it's a great way to spend some time practicing your putting.

Ask a Pro

There are loads of free games to play on smartphones or tablets. Ask an adult to go onto the App Store or Google Play, as there are sections dedicated to free games! Check age ratings and talk to your parents about which ones to try.

Introducing Skylanders

So many heroes!

In the very first *Skylanders* game, it was up to you to help them return to Skylands and save their home. Now, as a Portal Master, *you* are an amazing hero!

First appeared in: 2011
First game: Skylanders: Spyro's Adventure

....

The first game focused on Spyro the Dragon, but there were 32 figures to use. As a first-time Portal Master, you need to help the Skylanders return to the Skylands.

Abilities:

★ Fire-throwing
★ Water-launching
★ Magic
★ Strength
★ Flight
★ Stealth

Skylanders' top 3 characters

Stealth Elf

Stealth Elf has been in *Skylanders* games since the beginning, and she now appears in the Netflix TV series. She is sneaky, but also really powerful, too.

Wash Buckler

This octopus Skylander appeared in *Swap Force*, meaning you can pair him up with another character to combine skills!

Stormblade

Combine Stormblade with her vehicle, Sky Slicer, and it will be supercharged! This fast and powerful lark is really fun to use.

Keep them!

If you have some Skylanders figures from a previous game, they will work in the latest games, too. Make sure you keep them all!

Elemental

Each Skylander uses a different element, like Fire, Water, or Magic. You'll need certain elements to open up areas of each game.

Make your own

In *Skylanders Imaginators*, you can design your own Skylander. They're stored in crystals so you can show them off in friends' games, too.

Baddie buddies!

In *Trap Team* and *Imaginators*, you can use characters that are normally evil, like Kaos, to help the Skylanders!

Skylanders Academy is an animated TV show that you can watch on Netflix.

In *Skylanders Superchargers*, you will take part in driving levels and races.

Skylanders Imaginators

Create and play!

In *Skylanders Imaginators*, you create your own hero. There are millions of combinations, so you can make a unique creature with awesome skills.

Did you know?

Crash Bandicoot is one of the new Sensei characters in the game, and he has the highest attack stat of them all.

Highlight

Use your hero!

Once you've made your hero, you can guide them through the game's story and save the Skylands. As you play, you'll find new parts and weapons to power up your character more!

TOP 3 things to try

Create a hero

1 Create your own Skylanders from hundreds of different parts. Then, store them in the Creation Crystal to use again later! You can update your hero afterwards, too.

Explore the world

2 There are tons of cool places to discover in Skylands. Every level is unique, but you can also just explore Skylanders Academy and chat to your friends.

Play Creation Clash

3 In this tactical board game, you need to place stones on the grid to turn your opponent's stones to your color. It's easy at first, but it gets harder as you play!

TIPS & TRICKS

When you find a new character part or weapon, remember to use it! It'll increase your character's stats.

There are loads of things to collect in the game, from secret chests to Soul Gems. Grab everything!

You can take a selfie at any time, but if you find a Selfie Spot, you can take a really awesome photo!

Each element is strong against another, so think about your best choice for each new situation.

Skylanders Battlecast

Play your cards right!

If you love *Skylanders* and card games, *Battlecast* is for you. Play cards to summon characters, watch them fight, and outwit your opponents with a powerful deck.

Did you know?

There are over 60 missions to play through in the single-player Campaign mode.

Highlight

END TURN

Beat the boss!

When you come up against a powerful boss like Chef Pepper Jack, the battle will be tough. Outsmart him and you can strengthen your deck further!

260 TOP 3 coolest cards

60

BREAK
SPELL

Destroy an enemy gear o relic.

Break

1 If your opponent uses a powerful relic or piece of gear, use this card instead of wasting an attack to break it. Play it, then focus on doing some damage.

NETHER WARP
SPELL

Afflict an enemy character for 100 damage. Give it - 100 power until your next turn.

6

Nether Warp

2 It costs six crystals to play, but Nether Warp does a good amount of damage and will massively reduce your opponent's power.

TIPS & TRICKS

Make sure you build a deck that's balanced, with cards you can play cheaply and more powerful options.

If you can't use a card right away, think about how it might be useful later.

When your opponent uses a Relic card, focus on destroying it quickly to avoid bad effects.

Swap regularly between your three characters to play to their strengths.

FRUITS AND VEGGIES
SPECIAL ABILITY

Restore 10 health to a random ally. Shoot a random enemy for 10 damage.

1

Food Fight

3 This guy has a high Health stat, but also does a lot of damage. His special ability, Fruits and Veggies, heals a team member and damages opponents, making him a great team player.

Paper Mario: Color Splash

Flattened but still fun

The *Paper Mario* series has always been about clever puzzles, funny characters, and a cool battle system. *Color Splash* is no different, as Mario drops into a crazy world of paper and card for colorful adventures!

Highlight

Get cutting, Mario!

Cutout

When you find an area of the level that stands out, you can use the Cutout feature. Draw on the level using the Wii U Gamepad to reveal new areas!

TOP 3 activities

Paint the world!

1 In *Color Splash*, color has been drained from the world so everything is gray. Mario splashes paint around with his Magic Hammer to brighten it up.

Explore

3 There are lots of secrets to find In this beautiful paper world. Speak to everyone you meet—some of the things the characters say are hilarious!

> I'm no expert on bridge repairs, but I am an expert on bridge experts, and we're definitely gonna need one.

Battle

2 You will battle some classic Mario bad guys, including Koopas and Goombas. Be tactical and choose your moves carefully to win.

⏱ TIMELINE

2001
PAPER MARIO
Bowser trapped seven Star Spirits in playing cards, and it was up to Mario to save them. ⋯⋯⋯>

2004
PAPER MARIO: THE THOUSAND-YEAR DOOR
Mario searched for crystal stars to unlock a special door that hid a magical treasure. ⟨⋯⋯⋯

2007
SUPER PAPER MARIO
The evil Count Bleck opens a void that could destroy the universe, so Mario leaps into action! ⋯⋯⋯>

2012
PAPER MARIO: STICKER STAR
When Bowser touches a comet, it scatters powerful stickers across the world, which Mario must find.

LEGO Worlds

Brick by brick

L EGO *Worlds* gives you tools for mining and creating, and lets you loose to make whatever you want! There's no story mode here—just pure creation.

Did you know?

You can build huge creations in just a few seconds thanks to the game's building tools.

Highlight

Go big

With a little bit of planning, you can make huge things like this! When you're done, climb to the top of it and enjoy the view.

TOP 3 things to try

Build a house

1 You can build anything in LEGO *Worlds* using the building tool, whether it's a little house like this one or a huge castle with towers, battlements, and a drawbridge.

Did you know?

You can build vehicles like planes and boats to explore the world more easily.

Be anything

2 You can create your own character in LEGO *Worlds*! Become an astronaut, a racing driver, or even a dragon-riding wizard—the choice is yours.

Play with friends

3 You can play together on the same screen in multiplayer. So, build a racing track and you can race a friend. Or just explore the world together, and build.

TIPS & TRICKS

SAVE BUILDS

You can save your builds as Landscape Models. Rebuilding these saved models takes seconds.

COLLECT STUDS

Pick up all the LEGO studs you can. New items and bricks are unlocked with them!

RANDOMIZE

You can make your own character, but also try hitting Randomize to get a crazy creation.

GO HOME

If you get lost, you can go back to where you first started in your world from the pause menu.

Introducing Yoshi

Mario's cute dinosaur buddy!

He started out as a sidekick, but now, Yoshi is a hero in his own right. He's the star of his own games, as well as appearing in titles like *Super Smash Bros.* and *Mario Kart*.

First appeared in: 1991
First game: Super Mario World

Yoshi's playable debut was in the first *Mario* game for SNES, as a companion that Mario could ride. Yoshi was the hero of the sequel, *Super Mario World 2: Yoshi's Island*.

Abilities:
- ★ Egg laying
- ★ Egg throwing
- ★ Flutter jumping
- ★ Transformation
- ★ Keen sense of smell
- ★ Fire breathing
- ★ Eating

Yoshi's top 3 companions

Baby Mario

The aim of each stage in *Yoshi's Island* is to help Baby Mario reach the goal. Don't get hit, or Baby Mario will float off in a bubble!

Stars

These happy little things are everywhere in *Yoshi's Island*. Rescue them and they'll improve Baby Mario's bubble, giving you longer to rescue him.

Poochy

A helpful dog friend whose tough paws allow him to cross nearly any surface. Yoshi can ride him, too!

Yoshi

Rainbow Road
Green Yoshis are the most common, but they can also be found in a variety of other colors, too.

Dino might
Like Mario, Yoshi is shown to be extremely skillful. He can drive karts, play sports, and has even competed in the Olympics!

What a mouthful!
Yoshi's full name is actually T. Yoshisaur Munchikoopas, but don't worry—nobody ever calls him that!

Nintendo wanted to add a dinosaur buddy to 1985's *Super Mario Bros.*, but the NES hardware couldn't handle it.

Everything in *Yoshi's Woolly World* is made out of fabric. It all looks so soft and fluffy!

Yoshi's Island is a classic SNES game, but it's still lots of fun to play today.

Poochy & Yoshi's Woolly World

A hand-crafted adventure!

Yoshi's latest starring role is in this adorable knitted platform game. Everything is made out of wool, and you can use that to your advantage—eat enemies to create balls of yarn, craft your own platforms, or pull loose threads to reveal secrets!

Did you know?
Struggling to find secrets? Play in Mellow mode and Poochy-Pups will help you!

Did you know?
Nintendo used a similarly crafty art style for the excellent *Kirby's Epic Yarn*.

This is one of the cutest, most colorful games around!

Highlight

Burger Poochy

TRANSFORM!

There are lots of cool things that Yoshi can transform into by entering a Whirly Gate. They are all useful in their own way, so make sure you try them all out.

TOP 3
Yoshi abilities

Mermaid form

1 With this transformation, Yoshi is able to dive underwater. It also makes Yoshi attract nearby items, making it really useful!

Eating stuff

2 Yoshi's main way of dealing with enemies and obstacles is to eat things, turn them into balls of wool, and throw them around. He can eat just about anything!

Did you know?

Visit Yoshi Theater every day and you'll unlock short animations to enjoy.

Umbrella form

3 This strange ability is only used in a few sections, but it's really fun! You need to open and close Yoshi to ride air currents to the end of the level. Be careful not to fall!

TIPS & TRICKS

GRAB BEADS

These gem-like objects let you buy new Power Badges, so collect all that you see!

LOOK AROUND

Every level contains hidden secrets. If you see something suspicious, be sure to check it out!

EAT ALLIES

In the Wii U version, you can eat another Yoshi, then throw them to help them reach new areas.

Super Smash Bros.

Battle royale!

Who would win a battle between Mario, Pikachu, Kirby, and Sonic? Thanks to *Super Smash Bros.*, you can find out! Bring all your favorite gaming stars into the ring and duke it out to see who is the best character.

Did you know?

The first *Smash Bros.* game had just 12 characters. The latest games have nearly 60!

Grab the floating Smash Orb and you can use your most powerful attack, the Final Smash!

Highlight

All-stars!

Bringing together some of the biggest stars in gaming and watching them battle is one of the coolest things you'll get in any game!

TOP 3

alternative fighters

Wario

1 Wario is almost the opposite of Mario. He has a motorbike that can do a lot of damage to opponents, and he can use his bad breath to hurt them, too. Prepare for gas!

Did you know?
One of the bosses in the game is a pair of huge hands that can punch, grab, or poke you!

Fox McCloud

2 Fox is the hero of Nintendo's *Star Fox* series. He can dart around the screen and dash through opponents to damage them, and he has a laser.

Samus Aran

3 Samus's cool robotic suit is mainly for protection in the *Metroid* games. But here, she uses her cannon to shoot energy and rockets at opponents.

TIPS & TRICKS

DON'T MASH
Mashing the attack button over and over might do damage, but leaves you open to ranged attacks.

VARIATION
Each time you use the same move, it does a little less damage, so keep trying different things.

ROLL AROUND
Hold down the shield button and press a direction to perform a roll and get behind an opponent.

USE ITEMS
Items will appear on the level as you play. Grab them to do extra damage to opponents, or to heal yourself!

TOP 5
Hidden Gems

Try them out!

The big names, like *Mario*, *Pokémon*, and *Minecraft*, might get the headlines, but there are tons of amazing games out there to try.

1 Shovel Knight

2-D platformers have been making a comeback recently, and this is one of the best. It looks retro, and it's really fun, mixing testing jumps with great combat!

2 Ori and the Blind Forest

This side-scrolling platformer blends stunning graphics with awesome level design. It will really challenge your skills, and the story is amazing, too.

Did you know?

You can get a *Shovel Knight* amiibo, which adds co-op multiplayer to the Wii U version of the game.

3 Trackmania Turbo

High-speed racing doesn't get more extreme than *Trackmania*. You'll be racing up walls, driving upside down, and making insane jumps across the world at top speed. Awesome!

4 Stikbold!

This dodgeball title is a lot of fun. You can follow the weird story or just sit down with your friends and play with them on the same screen. Special skills and crazy characters make it really funny, too!

5 Abzû

Abzû is one of the most beautiful games you will ever play. It's an exploration game that lets you dive deep underwater, explore the ocean, and follow a powerful story.

Q & A

What's so special about Abzû?
Its simple controls and lack of on-screen information mean you're just free to explore the beautiful world. Swim with dolphins, experience the coral reef—whatever you like.

Is there a story?
Yes, although it's all explained through things you find. You'll notice robotic devices and find ruins buried in the sea. Figuring out what happened here is part of the fun.

Animal Crossing

Small town, big dreams

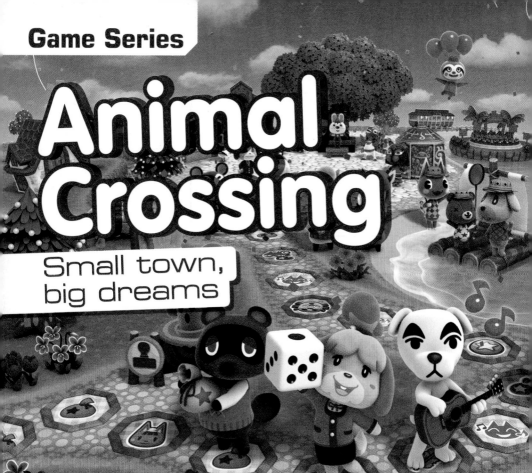

Animal Crossing games aren't action-packed. You move to a new village populated with animals, do some work, earn money, and improve your new home. It's a great chill-out game!

Did you know?

Mr. Resetti is a mole who shouts at you in the games if you turn them off without saving first.

Highlight

All yours

Be like a grown-up—pay off your debts, own your house, and have money in the bank. It feels great! Your house (and your town) will look really cool, too.

TOP 3
Animal Crossing games

1 New Leaf

You're the mayor of the town in this 3DS game. You can build things like benches and bridges to spruce the place up, play mini-games with friends, and customize your own character.

2 Animal Crossing

The first game in the series appeared way back in 2002. After you appear in a new town, you must work to pay back the money for your house ... and make some new friends!

3 amiibo Festival

This party game mixes up the *Animal Crossing* game, making it into a board game that you can play with friends. Your goal is to make your town the happiest and have fun!

TIPS & TRICKS

GET HELP
In *Happy Home Designer*, ask Lottie or Digby and they'll give you useful advice.

TIMING
In *New Leaf*, some items can be collected only at night, so make sure you play after dark sometimes.

AMIIBO!
Tap an amiibo to your device and you'll unlock new furniture, mini-games, and much more.

TRADING
Fruit that isn't native in your town will sell for more, so grow rarer plants if you can.

Mario Sports Superstars

Get in the game!

He might be famous for jumping and saving the princess, but Mario is a great sportsman, too. Over the years, he's done it all, from skiing to soccer, and he's back in action in *Mario Sports Superstars*!

Did you know?

There are five sports to play in *Sports Superstars*, including baseball and horse racing!

Highlight

Smash!

Hitting a winner in tennis is cool, but using one of your special shots to do it feels even better. Here, Peach smashes a great shot past Wario!

TOP 3 sports

Tennis

1 Much like the standalone *Mario Tennis* titles, this game mode includes special Ultra Smashes for each character to help them win the point.

Did you know?

You can choose from 18 playable characters, including Bowser, Yoshi, and Diddy Kong.

Golf

2 This chilled-out mode has you taking a trip around the golf course with Mario and friends. You can hit special shots, but this is most fun to play with friends.

Soccer

3 Here, you each take control of two players (like Luigi and Peach) on a team of 11, with the other players being Koopas or Shy Guys. Get ahold of the ball and try to score a goal!

⏰ TIMELINE

1999
MARIO GOLF 64
Mario's first 3-D sport game was a simple golf title. There were no special powers, just a fun game. ⋯⋯⋯⟩

2004
MARIO POWER TENNIS
Special courts and Power Shots brought tennis into the *Mario* world in style!

2008
MARIO SUPER SLUGGERS
Players used the Wii's motion controllers to hit the ball in this fun baseball game. ⋯⋯⟩

2011
MARIO SPORTS MIX

Mario and friends play dodgeball, ice hockey, basketball, and volleyball in this fun Wii title.

Slither.io

Eat it up!

If you just want to have a few minutes of fun, *Slither.io* is the ideal game. It's totally free to play, and easy to learn—although becoming a pro player is tougher than it looks. The goal is to get bigger by eating glowing orbs, but don't crash!

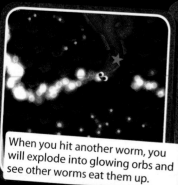

When you hit another worm, you will explode into glowing orbs and see other worms eat them up.

Highlight

Going to the top!

As you start to approach the top of the leaderboard, your hands might start to sweat. Don't make a mistake! Reach the top and you'll feel totally awesome.

TOP 3 skins

Rainbow

1 This is a great way to show off your colorful character. Switch to it and if you do eventually run into another player, you'll turn into multicolored glowing orbs.

Did you know?

There are other .io games available, including *Agar.io* and *Diep.io*, each with different game styles.

Cyclops

2 This is definitely the most monstrous skin offered in *Slither.io*. Its eye will follow your mouse cursor or finger around the screen as you play!

Antenna

3 We love the antenna skins because the little logo trailing from your worm's head wiggles around as you play and looks really funny. There are a few different design options, too.

TIPS & TRICKS

BOOST TIMING
Don't boost constantly! Stay in control and only boost when you really need to.

HANG AROUND
When you're small, find a big worm and stay close to them. If they crash, you can score big.

PLAN AHEAD
Don't rush into a bunch of worms and orbs—take your time and pick off your opponents.

CIRCLES
If you find a smaller worm, trap it in a circle and slowly make it smaller for a quick payout.

BEST MOBILE GAMES

Gaming on the go!

15 Skylanders SuperChargers

The Skylanders' adventure continues on your iPhone and iPad. Connect a Bluetooth Portal of Power to your device to play as characters in your collection, or choose a character in the game.

14 Despicable Me: Minion Rush

Minion Rush challenges you with new goals in each level. It has you sprinting through various locations collecting banana, using the touchscreen to jump and move around. The bonus games are lots of fun, too!

13 Scribblenauts Unlimited

Scribblenauts is a puzzle game with a difference—you can solve each puzzle using just about any item you can think of! Because this version is designed for smartphones and tablets, it's really easy to type out words and see the items appear on screen.

12 Forestry

This beautifully animated story has plenty of things to try. Whether you're feeding the animals, sorting bugs, or just taking a look around the forest to find things to play with, you'll never be bored.

11 LEGO Star Wars: The Force Awakens

Relive the epic adventures of *The Force Awakens* with the LEGO version of the movie on your tablet. Play as all your favorite characters and laugh as hilarious scenes tell the story.

10 Disney Crossy Road

In this game, you'll cross busy streets as all your favorite Disney characters, from Pumbaa to Buzz Lightyear. Unlocking new characters is great, and you can play this game with one finger!

9 Endless Alphabet

Practice your spelling with this cool game. Drag letters around the screen, then watch fun animations show you what each word means. The animations are cute—it's a great way to learn!

8 Sonic Dash

Can you keep up with Sonic? In this cool mobile twist on his usual adventures, the speedy hedgehog must grab rings, dodge hazards, and deal with powerful bosses, all with the help of your taps and swipes.

7 Rayman Adventures

Rayman is back with another 2-D action adventure! Use the Creatures you save to give you extra abilities as you sprint through levels and leap over obstacles using the touchscreen controls.

5 Super Mario Run

Mario makes his way to smartphones for the first time in this classic platformer. Jump through the levels to beat Bowser, compete with friends in Toad Rally, or just build up your Kingdom.

6 Explorium: Ocean for Kids

Explorium is all about—you guessed it—exploring the ocean floor and discovering cool creatures and awesome treasures as you go. Tap objects on the screen to find hidden mini-games and puzzles to solve while you travel through the deep blue sea.

3 Triple Town

It might look simple when you first start to play, but *Triple Town* is a puzzle game with hidden depth. Getting a high score isn't as easy as it first seems, and planning your moves is key. Always take time to think before you tap!

4 Pokémon GO

The game that captured the world's imagination has seen plenty of updates since it first launched. New Pokémon and special events encourage Trainers to keep exploring their local area safely to catch 'em all.

2 Toca Kitchen 2

Chop, season, and cook delicious meals for your guests in *Toca Kitchen 2*. This food-prep game has you slicing vegetables and blending mixtures with your finger, all to please your hungry friends! Get it right and they'll eat it up—but get it wrong and they won't be happy!

1 Minecraft: Pocket Edition

If you haven't already played *Minecraft* on smartphones and tablets, you don't know what you're missing. The mobile game is awesome, giving you access to a full *Minecraft* world complete with caves, tools, mobs, and more. Dive in and start mining!

Q & A

What do I need if I want to play these games?

All you need is a smartphone or tablet, like an iPad or an Android device. Most of the games will be available for both, so it doesn't matter which one you have.

How do I download them to my device?

Your smartphone or tablet will have an app store—open this and search for the game you want. Check with a grown-up that it's okay to download a game first, though.

Did you know?
....
You can buy an *Angry Birds* cookbook, which focuses on egg recipes from the piggies!

Angry Birds

Flying destruction!

This mobile gaming phenomenon is all about flinging birds at structures to knock them down. As well as their own games, the birds have starred in their own movie, and games themed around *Star Wars* and *Rio*!

Highlight

Perfect shot

Sometimes, you launch a bird perfectly, it lands exactly where you wanted, and the level crumbles in seconds. It's *Angry Birds* at its best!

TOP 3 birds

Red

1 The original, most famous, and angriest bird of them all, Red is a great all-arounder. Fling him at wood or glass and he's one of the best birds you can have.

Stella

2 Stella can create bubbles, which trap enemy piggies and loose blocks. She makes them float, then does tons of damage!

Silver

3 Silver is great at attacking hard-to-reach targets. When you tap the screen, she does a loop-the-loop and zooms straight down.

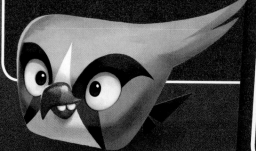

TIPS & TRICKS

COMPLETE QUESTS
Daily quests are the fastest way to earn gems in *Angry Birds 2*, so complete them whenever you can.

SAVE SPELLS
Angry Birds 2 features spells to help you through tough levels. Save them until you need them!

POINTS!
If you beat a level with birds left, you'll get a whopping 10,000 points for each!

ZOOM OUT
On your smartphone, you can pinch with two fingers to zoom out and see more of the level.

Introducing Ratchet & Clank

A hilarious duo!

What do you get when you mix platforming, fighting, robots, and space mammals? *Ratchet & Clank*, that's what! Engaging combat and funny characters have made this series a huge hit with gamers.

First appeared in: 2002
First game: Ratchet & Clank

Ratchet the Lombax meets up with Clank the robot, and they team up to stop the evil Chairman Drek from destroying whole planets!

Abilities:
- ★ Jumping
- ★ Zip-lining
- ★ Loyalty
- ★ Inventiveness
- ★ Fearlessness
- ★ Fighting
- ★ Piloting

Ratchet & Clank's top 3 games

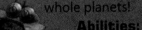

Ratchet & Clank

This game has been remade for the PS4, so you can now enjoy Ratchet & Clank's first adventure in HD!

A Crack in Time

The pair travel to the future, where Lombaxes are nearly extinct, and work together to save Ratchet's species.

Into the Nexus

This space-based game has the pair chasing down an intergalactic criminal, with some great platforming puzzles.

Ratchet & Clank

Legendary!

Ratchet's fighting skills are legendary—one character even claims he defeated the evil Tachyon with both hands tied behind his back and a stubbed toe!

Call him Clank

Ratchet calls him Clank, but the robot's official name is actually XJ-0461. It's the number he was given when he was first made.

Dance party

Ratchet's Groovitron weapon makes enemies dance uncontrollably. This is really funny, but also useful because it means you can take them out without them hurting Ratchet.

Ratchet often makes decisions quickly and can be a little rude. Clank balances him out by suggesting alternatives and being the voice of reason.

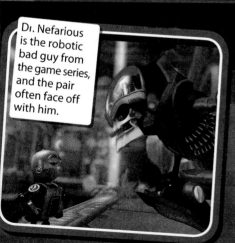

Dr. Nefarious is the robotic bad guy from the game series, and the pair often face off with him.

The latest game has been given a beautiful graphical update!

Ratchet & Clank

Relive the adventure!

Ratchet and Clank's latest adventure is actually a reimagining of the very first game, with new graphics. It's almost like a "Best Of" that brings the series up to date!

Did you know?

A *Ratchet & Clank* animated movie was released at the same time as the game in 2016.

Level up Ratchet's weapons and he'll have a better chance of beating tougher enemies.

Highlight

Graphical upgrade

The new game takes advantage of the PS4's power, with huge levels, amazing detail, and cool effects—especially when fighting enemies!

TOP 3 levels

1 Planet Kerwan

You'll start this level in your ship, flying around the skies of Kerwan. You need to suck up enemies and fire them back into their ships! You'll also unlock the Helipack upgrade.

2 Planet Aridia

This is a test of your platforming skills, with puzzles, moving platforms, and climbing sections. Plus, you'll discover a new tool here to empty and fill pools of water!

3 Nebula G34

The highlight of this level is the boss fight at the end of it, against the massive Blargian Snagglebeast. Watch out for the pools of deadly lava!

TIPS & TRICKS

EXTRA EXPERIENCE

If you die right at the end of a level, don't worry! Fight through the enemies again for more XP.

SAVE HEALTH

Don't break health crates if your HP is full. You can come back and get them later if you get hurt.

MIX YOUR WEAPONS

Keep switching weapons to level them up equally—don't rely on one.

PLAY AGAIN

You won't be able to grab all the hidden gold bolts in your first play through, so do it all again!

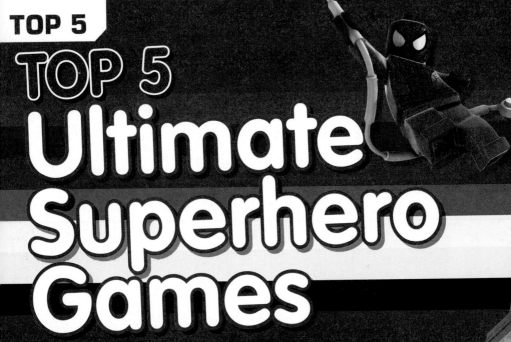

TOP 5
Ultimate
Superhero
Games

There's nothing better than a superhero game to help you feel like a star, whether you're swinging through a city as Spider-Man or stopping the Joker with Batman's help.

1 Scribblenauts Unmasked

In this puzzle game, you can use DC heroes like Batman to help you. Whether you're taking on a villain or just trying to climb a ladder, type in the name of any hero and they appear to help you!

Did you know?

Scribblenauts Unmasked features over 2,000 DC characters. Try typing in lesser-known ones, like Bouncing Boy and Awkwardman!

2 Marvel Pinball

You'll need to get high scores in this pinball game so the heroes leap into action. There are tons of table themes based on characters like the Avengers, Thor, and Spider-Man.

3 LEGO Batman 3: Beyond Gotham

Batman's third LEGO game has the Dark Knight and his friends fighting Brainiac. It's got epic action, more than 200 cool characters, and tough puzzles.

4 Mix+Smash: Marvel Super Hero Mashers

If you want a superhero experience on the go, try *Mix+Smash*. You can combine the arms, legs, torsos, and heads from different Marvel characters to create the ultimate hero and fight villains.

5 LEGO Marvel Super Heroes

Throw together over 130 of the coolest Marvel characters, an original plot, and a huge world to explore, and you've got one of the best superhero games ever.

Q & A

What's the story of LEGO *Marvel Super Heroes*?
When the huge space-creature Galactus comes to eat the Earth, the heroes of the Marvel universe must work together to gather Cosmic Bricks and stop him!

Can I be Iron Man?
Absolutely! There are several different versions of his armor to use, and they all have different abilities. You'll find well over 100 other characters. Some are heroes, and some are villains!

LEGO Marvel's Avengers

Avengers assemble!

Mixing together the stories of several of Marvel's films, LEGO *Marvel's Avengers* brings the coolest heroes together again. The stories are mixed with the classic LEGO humor, and the results are totally epic.

Did you know?

The game contains more than 200 playable characters to unlock using in-game studs!

Highlight

There are comic-book heroes in the game, too, like female Thor from the recent books.

Your favorite!

With so many heroes, your favorite is bound to be in there—we love Ms. Marvel! Find and unlock all of them!

TOP 3
coolest
characters

Hulkbuster

1 This huge suit has arc cannons, rockets, and lasers, to make it easy to disable enemies. Plus, thanks to the thrusters in the feet, it can fly around New York City and beyond.

Did you know?

If you rescue Stan Lee, who is stuck in every level, you'll unlock him as a character!

Vision

2 The coolest thing about Tony Stark's robot creation is his team-up moves. He can throw other characters around, and even throw Thor's hammer!

Captain America (Sam Wilson)

3 When Sam Wilson, AKA Falcon, takes over from Captain America, it's a big deal. He can fly, grapple, and— of course—he has Cap's shield, too.

TIPS & TRICKS

GET RED BRICKS
Replay levels in Free Play mode and use all your unlocked heroes to find the useful Red Bricks.

CHEAT CODE!
Pause the game and choose Input Code. Type in 5MZ73E to get the Fast Build cheat!

IRON STAN
Stan Lee combines the abilities of all the Avengers in one hero, so if you can unlock him, he's awesome.

SILVER CENTURION
To unlock Iron Man's Mk35 Silver Centurion suit, enter the code 4AKZ4G in the menu.

Super Mario Run

One-finger fun!

For the first time ever, Mario is on smartphone and tablet. Nintendo's all-new adventure can be controlled with just one finger. Tap away to make Mario jump!

Shop

New items have arrived!

300   300   300
0   0   0

As you earn coins and Toads, you'll be able to expand your Kingdom with buildings and decorations.

Highlight

Shelly
Winner!

Winner!

After you race through a Toad Rally level, you'll have to wait and see who has more coins, and more Toads. It's a tense few seconds, but if you win it will all be worth it!

? TOP 3
game modes

World Tour

1 You'll need to collect every coin you can to get the high score here. Find all five pink coins and the level will reset with new challenges and more difficult coins to find!

Did you know?

Speedrunners, who complete older *Mario* games super fast, were one of the inspirations for the game.

Toad Rally

2 This mode is all about style. Pull off cool jumps and feats of skill to attract more Toads and beat your friends' high scores, then take on the next friend on the leaderboard.

Kingdom Builder

3 When you've collected enough Toads, you can start to rebuild the kingdom that Bowser destroyed! Soon you'll have dozens of Toads living happily.

TIPS & TRICKS

LEARN IT ALL

Practice by playing levels over and over. Remember how each different jump you do works.

CHARACTER MIX

Choose different characters—characters like Yoshi have different jump styles to Mario!

TAKE A BREAK

When you find a pause block, the clock stops. Take a moment to plan!

BUY HOUSES

Save up Toads of different colors and buy special houses to unlock more characters!

Introducing Yooka-Laylee

Best friends working together!

Platformers don't come more colorful than *Yooka-Laylee*. The all-new 3-D adventure introduces us to Yooka the chameleon and Laylee the bat, who are on a mission to stop the evil Capital B!

First appeared in: 2017
First game: Yooka-Laylee

Yooka-Laylee is a brand-new game, with new characters. Yooka and Laylee travel through amazing levels, collecting all kinds of items, fighting enemies, and competing in races!

Abilities:
★ Jumping
★ Flight
★ Rolling
★ Snow-plowing
★ Fire-breathing
★ Sticky tongue

Yooka-Laylee's top 3 inspirations

Banjo-Kazooie
Many of the team worked on Banjo's platforming adventure. If you play it, you may spot just a few similarities to *Yooka-Laylee* . . .

Donkey Kong 64
Donkey Kong's first 3-D game introduced some crazy characters. It's a classic from way back in 1999!

Mario
Mario's adventures are the standard for all other platformers, mixing difficult jumps and boss battles.

A strong team

Some of the team that made *Yooka-Laylee* were also involved in gaming classics like *Banjo-Kazooie* and *Viva Piñata*.

Fly away

Laylee is the small purple bat that sits atop Yooka's head. She can fly around even with the chameleon dangling below.

Power-up!

Yooka has all kinds of abilities. He can breathe fire, grab items with his tongue, and even turn totally invisible!

The game was originally crowdfunded on Kickstarter. That just shows how many people wanted to play the game!

The game world looks great—it's built using the powerful Unity graphics engine.

This evil bee is the villain of the game, and he's called Capital B. Get it?

Yooka-Laylee

A colorful new adventure!

If you're looking for a fun new adventure, *Yooka-Laylee* is a great choice. This funny tale will test your platforming skills as you guide a chameleon and his bat buddy around.

Did you know?

The main collectible in the game is called a Pagie—it's a scroll that unlocks more levels.

Highlight

A whole new world

There are several different themed levels to unlock. Explore jungles, ice worlds, and even fairytale castles!

TOP 3
characters

Doctor Puzz

1 This scientist used to work with Doctor Quack, before he fired her and took all her work to the evil Capital B. Now Doctor Puzz helps Yooka and Laylee with upgrades.

Did you know?

You can find Shovel Knight, the hero from the game of the same name, in *Yooka-Laylee*.

Trowzer

2 You might not think a snake needs to wear pants, but Trowzer disagrees! He's a helpful reptile who will teach you new skills in exchange for the quills that you collect.

TIPS & TRICKS

Find the pirate ship and look for a nearby tree. Ground pound it to reveal a secret!

Hold down the crouch button for a couple of seconds and Yooka will do a super-high jump.

Kartos

3 Talking minecarts aren't really strange in the world of *Yooka-Laylee*. This one will let the duo jump in and take a crazy ride to collect gems on a minecart track.

Look for quills everywhere—they might be high up, in chests, or even underwater.

TOP 5
Coolest
Collectibles

Grab them all!

No matter what kind of game you're playing, you'll probably find that there's something to collect. Coins, rings, notes, or gems—there's usually something to find. Here are five of the best.

1 Imaginator parts

Skylanders Imaginators

There are over 1,000 Imaginators parts to collect in *Skylanders Imaginators*, by finding and opening chests. Each part has different stats.

Did you know?

With multiple color options for each individual Imaginator part in *Skylanders*, there are millions of creation options.

2 Red bricks
LEGO Marvel Super Heroes

Gold Bricks might be dotted all over LEGO *Marvel Super Heroes*, but Red Bricks are the ones you want. They'll give you special abilities, or even handy multipliers.

3 Pokémon
Pokémon Series

The excitement of finding new Pokémon to capture is awesome, and with over 800 cool creatures to collect, you've got a lot of work to do. When the Poké Ball stops wobbling, the Pokémon is yours!

4 Animals
Minecraft

You can domesticate lots of animals in *Minecraft*, and they're all useful. Wolves help you in battle, horses speed you up, and llamas will help you carry items.

5 Black Coins
Super Mario Run

Once you've got all of the pink and purple coins in *Super Mario Run*, black coins appear. These are tough to collect, so you need to be a master of the wall jump.

Q & A

Where are the black coins?
Each level has five, and they will be in hard-to-reach locations. They might be up high, or they might be hidden in "?" blocks that you need to headbutt.

Why should I bother with them?
Aside from the bragging rights, finding all 120 black coins will unlock a Black Coin Pipe that you can place in your Kingdom and use to access a special course.

Glossary

Achievement

An award you can unlock for completing a specific task on an Xbox console. This could include things like completing a level or beating a boss.

Beta

A small part of a game that the developers release early to let players test it. They use the tests to check that everything works properly.

Crowdfunding

Developers using public "pledges" rather than publisher investment to pay for making a new game.

Boss

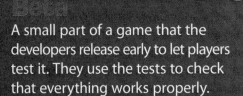

A tough enemy, usually found at the end of a level, that is bigger, tougher, and more powerful than the normal enemies that appear. Bosses often have a weak point that can be targeted.

Indie games

Games that are made by independent developers, usually with a small team.

Local multiplayer

Playing a multiplayer game with other people in the same room. Games like *Mario Kart* have modes that let you play locally.

Co-op

Co-op is a game mode in which you and others work together. You all have the same objectives, and work as a team to beat the game. It's short for "co-operative."

Mini-games

Quick challenges within a video game that will earn you bonuses if you win. Some games, like *Mario Party*, are based around these.

NPC

Non-playable character. These are characters around the game world that you can talk to and interact with, but not control.

Online multiplayer

Competing against other players via an Internet connection. You can add your friends to a list so you can play with them online.

Platformer

A type of video game that has you jumping across platforms to reach a final goal. 2-D platformers have players running from side to side, while 3-D platformers let you explore a full, 3-D world.

Skins

Personalized designs that you can put on your character to give yourself a unique look. In *Minecraft*, you can add a skin to your character to help you stand out from your friends.

Trophy

An award you can unlock for completing a specific task on PlayStation consoles. Trophies come in bronze, silver, gold, and platinum, depending on their level of difficulty.

Unlockable

Items or abilities that become available to you as you progress. You can unlock these by reaching a new level, buying them with in-game money, or finding them hidden in the world.

XP

Experience Points. Usually refers to in-game points that your character gains as you play. Earning a certain amount of points will cause your character to level up and become more powerful.